In This New Place
Poems

by Linda Marino

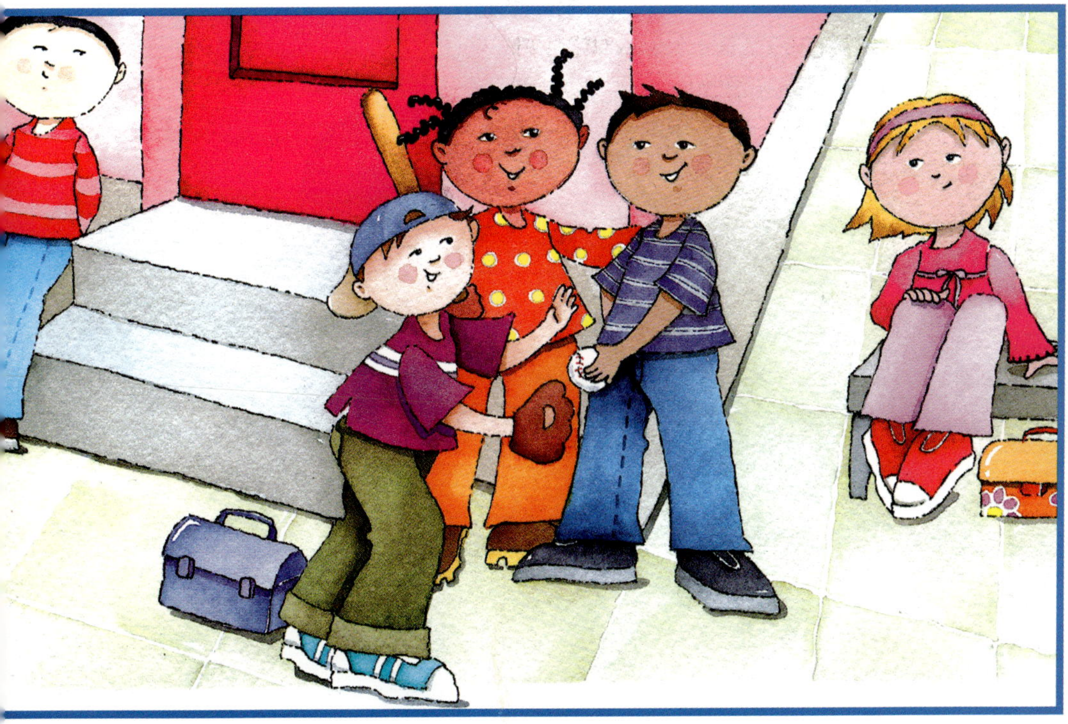

Illustrated by Rosario Valderrama

PEARSON
Scott Foresman

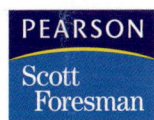

Editorial Offices: Glenview, Illinois • Parsippany, New Jersey • New York, New York
Sales Offices: Needham, Massachusetts • Duluth, Georgia • Glenview, Illinois
Coppell, Texas • Sacramento, California • Mesa, Arizona

Questions

Who is standing at my old window
This very moment, watching the sky?
Who is watching the shadows I saw
Change on the grass as the day goes by?

What's in my room now, where my things were?
Is there a trace of what was there?
Is there a tiny trace of me
Standing there too, watching the tree
Cast its long shadows on the lawn?
What is the place like—with me gone?

Where Am I From?

They want to know.
Where am I from?
Mexico. India. Vietnam. Poland.
You try to look like the other kids.
You pay attention to how they talk.
You listen on the playground and realize
That they say "Come ear," and not "Come here,"
That they say "Wanna," and not "Want to,"
That they don't speak English the way your mother
   does—
English she learns in the class at night
In the library.

---

pay attention to: observe, notice

You look in the mirror.
Where am I from?
And your heart beats for the country you knew,
And your head is full of the songs you hear,
When you come in from school, and the radio
Is playing loud, as your mother cooks.
And your eyes are dark like the land you left
Or light like the sky or river there.
Where am I from? You ask yourself,
And you think of the voices:
"Come ear, come ear!"

In This New Place

In this new place, I will admit
I miss the place where I used to fit,
Where I belonged, like air, like light—
It wasn't perfect, but it was right.

In this new place I barely see
The things that are in front of me.
My eyes look back to what I knew—
It wasn't perfect, but it was true.

In this new place, I will hold fast
To what I had, and let time pass.
New air, new light, against my skin,
New life around, to take me in,
In this new place, in this new time—
It isn't perfect, but it's mine.

---

miss: feel the absence of something or someone
fast: firmly

pizza

BLT sandwich

Cafeteria Menu, First Time Around

"Pizza" I understand. Okay, pizza is served every day.
But a hero sandwich? What does that mean?
Will a tiny man in a cape appear
Pushing through lettuce
So glad he met us?
Oh, what an episode that would be!
My mind fills with wonder! And a BLT?
There are so many things that sandwich could be!
And a club sandwich? Can non-members eat it?
And what is this 'n in "beef 'n beans"?
And what is a "RibBQ"?
Oh, soon I will know what it all means,
But right now I'm not sure what to do.
That pizza smells nice—
Should I have a slice?
No! I must try new things!
Let's see what that hero brings!

---

cape: a piece of clothing that hangs from the shoulders, like the cloth on a cartoon superhero's back

Extend Language | **Regional Words**

People in different regions of the United States use different words for the same thing. For example:

There are many words for a sandwich that is made with two slices of crusty bread (about six inches long) and filled with meats, cheeses, pickles, and other ingredients. In Philadelphia, this kind of sandwich is called a *hoagie*. In the Northeast, it is called a *grinder* or a *sub,* and in the South, it is called a *poor boy*. This kind of sandwich also can be called a *hero,* an *Italian sandwich*, a *submarine,* and a *torpedo.*

Why do you think some foods or meals have different names in different regions of the country?

hero sandwich

Supply List for a New Student

One combination lock,
Five blue pens—
A little bit of courage
To make new friends.
A ruler that marks inches
And centimeters, too.
A lot of knowing who you are
And all that you can do
A scientific calculator,
Notebooks for each class—
A good supply of hope
That lonely times will pass.

combination lock

spiral notebooks

ruler